UNDERSTANDING
YOUR **DIVINE**
CALLING & PURPOSE

Understanding Your Divine Calling And Purpose
All Rights Reserved

Copyright © 2016 by Victor Owusu-Teng

No part of this publication may be reproduced, stored in a retrieval system or transmitted in any way by any means, electronic, mechanical, photocopy, recording or otherwise, without the prior written permission of the author except as provided by USA copyright law.

All Bible references are taken from the New King James Version, unless otherwise stated.

Author's Contact: *vowusut@gmail.com*

The opinions expressed by the author are not necessarily those of Rehoboth House.

Paperback: 978-1-68411-254-8
Hardcover: 978-1-68411-254-5

Published in the United States of America by
Rehoboth House, Chicago.
rehobothhouseonline.com

Table of Contents

Dedication ix

Foreword xiii

Introduction xix

Chapter 1
Defining Purpose 1

Chapter 2
Vision And Mission 15

Chapter 3
Defining The Call 29

Chapter 4
What Comes With The Calling? 43

Chapter 5
You Are Not An Accident 59

Conclusion 77

Dedication

With great pleasure and privilege, my wife and I dedicate this book; *"Understanding Your Divine Calling And Purpose"* to our dearly father and mother, Rev. Dr. Stephen K. Gyermeh and Mrs. Comfort Gyermeh. Rev. Dr. Stephen K. Gyermeh is the General Overseer and Founder of The Church of The Living, with headquarter in Hyattsville, MD, USA, and other branches across USA and the world over.

God in His mercy, handpicked him from an idolatrous and heathen home at the age of sixteen. Immediately after his conversion to the Lord and water baptism by immersion, Dr. Stephen K. Gyermeh was immediately baptized and filled with the Holy Spirit at that tender age of his life. Ever since, he has preached the Gospel and taught the impregnable and infallible Word of God without compromise. He has traveled across the globe, from town to town, and city to city, country to country, continent to continent, preaching in jails and prisons in United States. Under his ministry, many have come to know the Lord Jesus Christ and have received raw miracles and physical healings from tumors, cancer, arthritis and other diseases. The dead have been raised to life in the ministry of Rev. Dr. Stephen K. Gyermeh over the years.

He has raised great men and women who are firebrand preachers of the Gospel. Rev. Dr. K. Gyermeh has a passionate desire and a compassionate heart for the Body of Christ.

Rev. Dr. Stephen K. Gyermeh is blessed with a wonderful wife, Mama Comfort Gyermeh.

They have four wonderful children totally sold out to God, as workers in the vineyard: Pastor Samuel, Minister Daniel, Sister Joana and Minister Esther, and also they are blessed with eleven grandchildren. Rev. Dr. Stephen K. Gyermeh has also raised many sons and daughters in the vineyard of God. He has also authored many books and his latest books are:

- *The Miracles of God*
- *Marriage in The Biblical Way*
- *The Works of the Devil and the Christian Warfare.*

Beloved, considering the life of this man of God (Rev. Dr. Stephen K. Gyermeh) and his active involvement in ministry today even at his old age, you will agree with me that this is a man who understands his divine calling and purpose, and he is actively fulfilling it. His consistent commitment and passion for the Kingdom are contagious and worthy of emulating. This is an enduring godly legacy.

Understanding Your Divine Calling And Purpose

Foreword

Pastor Victor Owusu-Teng is a young energetic Servant of God who has soul-winning at the core of his ministry as evidenced in this book. He is very compassionate for people and passion for ministry. He attends to referrals made to him by fellow ministers and others with a sense of urgency. He believes that as Christians, we have been saved to save others, loved to love others, and delivered from the shackles of the enemy to deliver others. Ephesians 5:7-14 captures the heart cry of Pastor Victor because many Men and Women of God are gradually failing to understand their Divine Calling and

Purpose so he sounds a timely caution to the church and says,

> *"Awake, sleeper, and arise from the dead. And Christ will shine on you" (Eph. 7:14).*

Pastor Victor reminds the reader of God's Word in Jeremiah 29:11- *"For I know the plans I have for you, declares the Lord, plans to prosper you and not to harm you, plans to give you hope and a future".*

In context, the author tells the reader that like the Prophet Jeremiah, we were all born from a particular precious and honorable womb, on a specific date and at a specific location, with a specific divine assignment to fulfill. Regardless the challenges and seeming past or current failures in life, the plan, calling, and purpose of God cannot fail but succeed to glorify God. Your family background, education, career and training, difficulties and difficult people in your life are all part of a divine plan that is unfolding to equip you fully for the manifestation of your purpose in this life. Pastor Victor quoted **Dr. Myles Munroe**, an International Preacher from the Bahamas who has gone to be with Lord in the words "Your existence is evidence that this generation needs something that your life contains."

Touching on experimentation and copying other ministers in response to their calling, Pastor Victor highlights the offices of the Fivefold Ministry Gifts in Ephesians 4:11 and pleads with Christians to "stay in their own spiritual lanes" and not to cross to other "lanes" not meant for them. If the we disobey this simple and passionate plea, abuses in ministry become the ultimate outcome. The Word of God in Proverbs 19:21 supports the author's plea- *"We humans keep brainstorming options and plans, but God's purpose prevails."*

I am personally touched by what **Dr. Myles Munroe** once said- "The wealthiest places in the world are not gold mines, oil fields, diamond mines or even banks. The wealthiest place is the cemetery. There lie companies that were never started, masterpieces that were never painted. In the cemetery, there is buried the greatest treasure of untapped potential. There is a treasure within you that must come out. Don't go to the grave with your treasure still within YOU." This quote gives us an impressionistic view of what this timely book is about.

Pastor Victor is an anointed young man who has a network of other pastors and Christian friends and he humbly learns from them, and they, also learn from him. He occasionally brings some of them to minister at their prayer conference and church, the Church of the Living God in Chicago. I have such a high respect for Pastor Victor and his team of leadership and church members, who are very much Kingdom-minded. This is a particular church I can confidently recommend to anyone looking for a home church.

Foreword

Pastor Victor is a loving and caring husband to his dearest wife, Mrs. Georgina Owusu-Teng, who stands solidly behind him in ministry. He is also a disciplined and caring father to their children; Abigail, Aaron, Anna, and Ame. He therefore passes the test conducted by the Apostle Paul in 1 Timothy 3:5- For if a man cannot manage his own household, how can he take care of God's church?

Pastor Victor, congratulations!

I am deeply honored and privileged to write the foreword to this more than timely book.

Chaplain Dr. Gabriel Amoateng-Boahen
Professional Staff Chaplain (Retired)
University of Chicago Medical Center
Chicago, Illinois USA.

Understanding Your Divine Calling And Purpose

Introduction

History has repeatedly proven that most of the times God choses people who are lightly esteemed by all human standards to accomplish great and divine assignments on earth. Often, He uses ordinary individuals with no reputation to reckon with to build and expand His Kingdom to the amazement of the world.

> *"For ye see your calling, brethren, how that not many wise men after the flesh, not many mighty, not many noble, are called. But God hath chosen the foolish things of the world to confound the wise; and God hath chosen the weak things of the world to confound the things which are mighty" (1Cor1:26-27 KJV).*

God in His divine providence and infinite wisdom, rarely uses famous people like celebrities, aristocrats, the royalties and upper echelon of the world in accomplishing His plans on earth. Though He can if He decides to, but in rare occasions. By all standards, God's criteria are different from the criteria of the world. As Isaiah 55:8 says,

"For my thoughts are not your thoughts, neither are your ways my ways" saith the Lord of hosts."

With this insight from the above scripture comes these critical questions that will be answered in chapters three and four as we make progress in this journey.

Who is called?
Who are you called to?
Where are you called to?
What comes with the call?
How do you respond to the call?
What is the qualification to be called?

Introduction

I encourage you to allow the Lord to teach you beyond what is written in this book.

Dear reader, my utmost and sincere desire is that after reading and digesting the content of this book, you will have a deeper and better understanding of the call of God upon your life and how to respond accordingly.

I want to reiterate that God has repeatedly chosen people who were lightly esteemed by the world's standard to accomplish great feats for His Kingdom. As we progress further in this study, we will understand why He most often uses ordinary people like some of us reading this book to do great things on earth.

It will further validate Apostle Paul's letter to the Corinthian brethren.

> *"For you see your calling, brethren, that not many wise according to the flesh, not many mighty, not many noble, are called. But God has chosen the foolish things of the world to*

put to shame the wise, and God has chosen the weak things of the world to put to shame the things which are mighty" (1 Corinthians 1:26-28 NKJV).

Two Examples of Ordinary People Used Mightily by God

"It is yet to be seen what God would do through one man's life surrendered totally to Him. I determine to be that man", said **D. L Moody. Moody.**

Moody was never ordained by man but was used mightily by God to impact three continents with the power of God working through his life. His conviction was that *"… all things are possible to those that believe" (Mark 9:23).*

Moses grew up with the pride and arrogance of the Egyptian Monarchy as a Prince. He was the son of Pharaoh's daughter. For him to be qualified to shepherd God's people, God allowed circumstances of life to drive him to the wilderness, where He purged him of all the wisdom, fame and pride of Egypt. Moses cascaded from presiding over the nobles in the Royal Palace of Pharaoh to watching and presiding over sheep in the Arabian desert for forty years.

Forty years in the wilderness transformed the haughtiness of Moses to humility and his hostility to harmony. Afterward, God empowered him with His wisdom and might that the Egyptian Kingdom could not match. All his intellectual and military training in Egyptian was insufficient to save and deliver the children of Israel out of the bondage of Pharaoh. Amazingly, after an encounter with God in the burning bush, with an ordinary shepherd's rod in his hand, he could deliver an entire nation from the iron claws of the strongest king at the time.

> *The LORD said to him, "What is that in your hand?" And he said, "A staff" (Exodus 4:2).*

Again, in spite of all his training and exposure to the Egyptian system and access to the resources and wealth of Pharaoh, Moses could not deliver the children of Israel out of bondage. It was an encounter with Jehovah in the Desert of Median that changed the equation and drew the battle line. It was God's anointing during the encounter in the burning bush that turned him into an anointed shepherd to fulfill the call of God on his life.

That single encounter with the Lord God Jehovah, led Moses to discover and perfectly understand God's purpose for his life, which was the reason he was born and preserved when Pharaoh killed all male children within his age bracket in Egypt. The divine purpose for this anointed shepherd was to deliver the children of Israel from the hands of Pharaoh. He could accomplish that divine purpose only after he submitted to God's master plan for his life. The same principles apply to everyone of us today.

Genesis 46:34 says,
> *"That you shall say, 'Your servants' occupation has been with livestock from our youth even till now, both we and also our fathers,' that you may dwell in the land of Goshen; for every shepherd is an abomination to the Egyptians."*

Lessons Learned

It does not matter how perfect your plans are, if they do not line up with the divine plan and purpose of God for your life, you will end up moving in cycle and returning to the same starting point. Consequently, frustration and agitation become bedfellows in your life, because you never knew or either ignored God's divine purpose for your life. In every aspect of life, when the purpose of a thing is not known, abuse becomes inevitable. What a tragic experience!

Purpose in the context of our discussion means knowing and understanding what you were born to accomplish. However, you need a well defined vision to carry out your purpose. Thus, vision is the ability to see ahead of your clear purpose and begin to imagine the necessary practical work towards its fulfillment, once you understand your purpose and remain committed to fulfilling it, God will help you accomplish it. All you need to do at this stage in your life is to streamline the things you do and channel your resources and time only to those things that will eventually translate into accomplishing God's purpose for your life.

> *"And we know that all things work together for good to them that love God, to them who are the called according to his purpose" (Romans 8:28).*

Looking at world history and the consistency of Scriptures, you will realize that God does not consider the social status of people as a precondition for calling them. That explains why He rarely uses the cream and upper class in the society, like kings, queens, politicians, scientists, great philosophers, renown professionals, movie stars and other celebrities to advance His Kingdom, though He can if He chooses to and occasionally does, don't get me wrong. Our God has the ability, the capacity, the right and the resources to use anybody He chooses to. The decision to use anyone He wants to is solely His prerogative and no one can question Him.

> *"Behold, I am the Lord, the God of all flesh. Is there anything too hard for Me?" (Jeremiah 32:27).*

Understanding Your Divine Calling And Purpose

CHAPTER 1
Defining Purpose

The word purpose can be defined as the reason, the motivation, the basis, or the cause for which something exists. Purpose justifies why something is created, done, or better still, undone. Purpose precedes the creation of anything.

"Your existence is evidence that this generation needs something that your life contains" – **Dr. Myles Munroe.**

Purpose in the context of our discussion is about knowing and understanding who you are in the Lord (your identity), and everything that comes with your identity as a Christian. It is about knowing your inheritance in Christ, reserved and prepared for you before you were born. God designed your purpose, with the intent to enable you to accomplish what you were born to do. Indeed, you can only fulfill your purpose if you know who you are in Christ and the enormous resources available at your disposal, in Him.

For you accomplish your purpose, you need a distinct vision and a clearly stated mission statement. Vision is the ability to see your God-given purpose beyond the natural eyes. With a clear-cut vision, you can see and imagine the fulfillment of your purpose in your mind. Then, the mission is how to get it done with the available divine resources and helpers prepared for you. As we read on, I will expound further on mission and vision in the next chapter.

It is imperative to clearly understand that as we embark on the journey to fulfilling the purpose of God for our lives, God will often use the circumstances and crises of life to reposition us to see and maximize our potential, thereby moving us into the great accomplishment of the purpose we were born to fulfill. However, at such times, it's important to discern if God is at work in your life or the devil is taking undue advantage of the situation to attack you. The devil's ultimate goal is to eventually discourage and dissuade us from our journey to fulfill our God-given purpose.

Do not be terrified or allow your problems to subdue you and becloud your vision. Rather, be stirred up by your dreams and forge ahead to the finishing line. Endeavor to see your God-given vision come to fruition, within the specified time frame God apportioned for you. Knowing that you have a spiritual treasure in your earthen vessel at such times, propels you to press on against all the odds, towards the finishing line to fulfill your God-given purpose.

> *"But we have this treasure in earthen vessels, that the excellence of the power may be of God and not of us. We are hard-pressed on every side, yet not crushed; we are perplexed, but not in despair; persecuted, but not forsaken; struck down, but not destroyed"*
> *(2 Corinthians 4:7-9 NKJV).*

God's wants us to realize that everything valuable to us in this life came from Him, and furthermore embrace the fact that He has a unique plan and purpose for everyone, as we see a typical example in Jeremiah 1:4-5:

> *"Then the word of the LORD came unto me, saying, Before I formed thee in the belly I knew thee; and before thou camest forth out of the womb I sanctified thee, and I ordained thee a prophet unto the nations"*
> *(Jeremiah 1:4-5).*

The purpose of God for your life is your unique gifts and talents that must be defined and refined. By refining them, you are making room to express your gifts and talents in the world. The more refined your gifts and talents, the more in demand you will be.

Further, Jeremiah 29:11 tells us that,

> *"For I know the thoughts that I think toward you, saith the LORD, thoughts of peace, and not of evil, to give you an expected end."*

According to Dr. Myles Munroe, people fall into one of these three groups:

- **The few who make things happen**
- **The many who watch things happen**
- **The overwhelming majority, who have no notion of what is happening**

Sincerely ask yourself, where do I belong to among these three categories? Your answer to this question determines the disposition of your life. It's a matter of choice and destiny. Remember that we are governed by the daily decisions we make. Unavoidably, you live with whatever decision you make in life, until you decide otherwise. If your decisions are influenced by God's purpose for your life, you will live a focused and streamlined life.

Every person is either a creator of fact or a creature of circumstance. You either add color into your environment or like a chameleon, takes color from your environment.

I pray that God shall completely dismantle every opposition that may attempt to hinder your effectiveness in fulfilling His plans for your life. It could be your job, your friends, your career, your family, your ideologies, your possessions, your perception of life, your personal accomplishments, name it. If it conflicts and attempts to thwart God's plans for your life, He will ultimately move them out of your life, to pave a way for His plans to prevail in your life

> *"We humans keep brainstorming options and plans, but God's purpose prevails" (Proverbs 19:21 TMB).*

Dr. Myles Munroe said, "The wealthiest places in the world are not gold mines, oil fields, diamond mines or banks. The wealthiest place is the cemetery. There lie companies that were never started, masterpieces that were never painted. In the cemetery, there is buried the greatest treasure of untapped potential. There is a treasure within you that must come out. Don't go to the grave with your treasure still within YOU."

Examples of Fulfilled Purposes

Paul:

> *"For I am now ready to be offered, and the time of my departure is at hand. I have fought a good fight, I have finished my course, I have kept the faith: Henceforth there is laid up for me a crown of righteousness, which the Lord, the righteous judge, shall*

give me at that day: and not to me only, but unto all them also that love his appearing" (2 Timothy 4:6-8 KJV).

David:

"For David, after he had served God's will and purpose and counsel in his own generation, fell asleep [in death] and was buried among his forefathers, and he did see corruption and undergo putrefaction and dissolution [of the grave]" (Acts 13:36 AMP).

Jesus:

*"After this, Jesus, knowing that all things had already been accomplished, to fulfill the Scripture, *said, "I am thirsty." A jar full of sour wine was standing there; so they put a sponge full of the sour wine upon a branch of hyssop and brought it up to His mouth. Therefore, when Jesus had received the sour wine, He said, "It is finished!" And He bowed His head and gave up His spirit"* (John 19:28-30 NASB).

May we become like Apostle Paul, King David, Prophet Daniel, Joshua, Mary, Esther, Deborah and ultimately the Lord Jesus, who fought the good fight, finished their course, kept their faith, and emptied themselves for their generations and beyond.

"Solid character will reflect itself in consistent behavior, while poor character will seek to hide behind deceptive words and actions. **Dr. Myles Munroe.**

Our Inheritance and Heritage in Christ
Heritage is important because it speaks of your origin. If you know where you came from, you will know where you are going. This woman in the Scripture seems not to know her heritage in Abraham; thus Satan robbed her of her heritage of divine healing and health, and consistently tormented her with the spirit of infirmity for eighteen years.

"But the synagogue official, indignant because Jesus had healed on the Sabbath, began saying

to the crowd in response, "There are six days in which work should be done; so come during them and get healed, and not on the Sabbath day." But the Lord answered him and said, "You hypocrites, does not each of you on the Sabbath untie his ox or his donkey from the stall and lead him away to water him? "And this woman, a daughter of Abraham as she is, whom Satan has bound for eighteen long years, should she not have been released from this bond on the Sabbath day" (Luke 13:14-16)?

It has rightly been said that the only weapon the enemy has against us is ignorance and lies. His battle is only effectual as long as he can repeat the lies again and again until it sounds like the truth. Our weapon against the lies of the devil is the Truth of the Word of God rightly applied in our lives.

Throughout the Scriptures, God promises to bless His people. However, many believers do not know the glorious blessings God promised them. Hosea 4:6 tells us that many perish due to a lack of knowledge. This verse is true when it comes to knowing the specific blessings that God promises His people because of His commitment to His covenants. As a result, many believers do not experience the full benefits of what they are promised in their relationship with Christ.

Imperatively, there are spiritual connections between God's blessings and His covenants with us. His unfailing covenant promise is a guarantee to every redemptive blessing we have in Jesus Christ. God interacts with man through His unfailing covenants. We must live with the consciousness that God is a covenant-making and covenant-keeping God. Because of this, every blessing promised by God is only made available through His covenant promises and conditions.

To live and experience the reality of God's blessings, it is imperative that we understand the depth and breadth of God's covenants. Covenant is the foundation from which every promise in the Bible depends on and is the reason why God's blessings flow into our lives. God's covenants and His blessings are so closely connected. As already mentioned, God's blessings are based upon His covenants with man. In fact, His covenant is how we know that God is committed to blessing us. Even more importantly, a covenant is the means by which we get a hold on God.

To see why covenant is so important to knowing that God will bless us. Let us look at the promises of blessing that God made to Abram, who later became Abraham.

> *"Now the LORD had said unto Abram, get thee out of thy country, and from thy kindred, and from thy father's house, unto a land that I will shew thee: And I will make of thee a great nation, and I will bless thee, and make thy name great; and thou shalt be a blessing: And I will bless them that bless thee, and curse him that curseth thee: and in thee shall all families of the earth be blessed" (Genesis 12:1-3).*

What was the great Apostle Paul actually talking about when he brought up the topic of inheritance in his epistles?

> *"In him we have obtained an inheritance, having been predestined according to the purpose of him who works all things according to the counsel of his will, so that we who were the first to hope in Christ might be to the praise of his glory. In him you also, when you heard the word of truth, the gospel of your salvation, and believed in him, were sealed with the promised Holy Spirit, who is the guarantee of our inheritance until we acquire possession of it, to the praise of his glory" (Ephesians 1:11-14 ESV).*

He was pointing out God's inheritance and our inheritance in Christ to the brethren then, as well as to us today. This scripture is as relevant as it was to them, and as it is to us today and ever shall remain.

> *"But the word of the Lord endures forever." Now this is the word which by the gospel was preached to you" (1 Peter 1:25 NKJV).*

Understanding Your Divine Calling And Purpose

Chapter 2

Vision And Mission

Vision is the ability to see beyond now. It stretches out into the future and articulates how you plan to execute your God-given purpose. Vision embodies and spells out the plan, the strategy, and the blueprint of the whole purpose or call of God on your life.

The greatest tragedy in life is having sight but lacking vision (the ability to see beyond the physical). If you do not see where you are going, you will never get there, because your destination will remain elusive. Therefore, if you don't know where you're going, no road or route will take you there. Vision is the compass you need to get to your destiny in life.

Your Global Positioning System (GPS) will not give you a final destination if you do not know your point of origin and your intended destination. You have to program your destination into the device.

Effective leaders in any organization must have the ability to unambiguously define and precisely communicate the vision of the organization they are leading, if they must be successful as leaders. The ability to articulate the vision is a core component of successful leadership. Typically, vision and mission statements should summarize an organization's goals and how to accomplish it. It lays out the strategies in ways that can be effectively communicated and easily understood by those who believe in the vision. The more concise and precise you are in defining the vision, the more chances of understanding it.

Vision statement

A vision statement clearly and concisely sets out the ministry or company's short and long-term goals and aspirations. The intent of a vision statement is to inspire, motivate and galvanize the ministry or company's workforce, by providing a picture of where the organization is heading to.

It also provides a reality check for leaders, to periodically compare their strategic objectives and operational plans with the vision statement. If at any time a planned course of action does not move the ministry or company toward its vision, it may be necessary to revisited and possibly revised the vision statement. A vision statement is a major step in creating a culture of language that embodies why your organization exists, and what it is committed to accomplishing.

Mission Statement

Mission statements are important steps in creating the language that embodies why your ministry exists and what it is committed to accomplishing for the Kingdom of God. Making promises in a mission statement is not relevant, because the mission statement should reflect the reason why we do the things we do and how we do them.

Indeed, in the corporate world, a mission statement defines a company's values, goals, ethics, culture, and the norms for making decisions that affect the overall objectives of the organization. It summarizes what the company does, why they do the things they do, and how they do them. It also sets out how the company conducts its day-to-day business and identifies key stakeholders of the organization, such as shareholders, customers, employees and the general public.

A mission statement also helps employees to understand where their contributions fit into the company's objectives. It also helps other stakeholders decide whether they want to do business with the organization or not.

Identity and Destiny

Knowing who you are in the Lord Jesus Christ will determine how you arrived at your appointed place. This is a place where you will eventually be planted, decorated, owned and never again be tossed or pushed around in life.

> *"Moreover I will appoint a place for My people Israel, and will plant them, that they may dwell in a place of their own and move no more; nor shall the sons of wickedness oppress them anymore, as previously" (2 Sam 7:10 NKJV).*

If you do not know who you are, others will define and label you as they wish or think. God has put a mark on you, not only in the natural but also in the spiritual realm, which defines your identity in Christ.

In Acts 19, a group of exorcists, whom the Bible identifies as the seven sons of a man named Sceva, attempted to cast an evil spirit out of a demon-possessed man. But when they commanded the evil spirit to come out of that man, the spirit answered them:

> *"... Jesus I know, and Paul I know; but who are you? Then the man who had the evil spirit jumped on them and overpowered them all. He gave them such a beating that they ran out of the house naked and bleeding" (Acts 19:14-16).*

Think of it; the evil spirit in the man knew who Jesus and Paul were. Even though Paul lived in a small physical body that had been mercilessly beaten, bruised and abused, but he was so powerful in the spiritual realm that hell knew his name.

Do you know who you are in Christ and does the devil also know your identity in Christ? Perhaps, the limitations of Apostle Paul's flesh turned out to be to his greatest advantage. Because he could not lean on his flesh, he had to learn how to function in the realm of the spirit, and that's the reason the evil spirit knew who he was.

Apparently, great family background, tribe of origin, credentials, life accomplishments, marriage, education, church membership, financial status, friends, children, social class and physical muscles can make you look great in the natural, but mere flesh and blood have no effect on the devil or the spiritual realm.

Regardless of how you look in the physical realm, you are a menace to the devil in the spiritual realm, if you know who you are in Christ. In that realm, you are anointed and powerful, with the ability to pull down strongholds in the kingdom of the enemy. You are mighty and powerful in Christ that the devil and his forces know you and flee from you, when you resist them in Jesus' name.

To comprehend your divinely assigned destination in life, you have to know who you are in the Lord. Some people have failed and are defeated in life because they allowed the circumstances of life, their past experiences and the opinions of other people to decide and define their identity. If you have misplaced identity, it can limit your ability to see and reach your appointed destination, thereby inhibiting you to fulfill your God-given purpose.

To be ignorant of your identity can cause you to settle for little and less than your best. Misplaced or ignorance of your identity can diminish your very existence and ability to take charge and dominion of your domain (ministry, career, business, academics,) and every other endeavor of life that God has positioned you to excel.

In Ecclesiastes. 10:7 the preacher tells us that princes are walking on foot and servants are riding on horses. What it means is that, because of lack of understanding and clue of their identity in the kingdom, it has woefully resulted to influential people walking on foot like slaves, while slaves with knowledge are riding and sitting on horses like kings. Ignorance can cost you dearly in life, ministry, business, and finances.

Your ignorance will ultimately give the devil undue advantage over you, to the extent that it could prevent you from exercising your supreme authority and dominion in Christ Jesus over him.

2 Corinthians 2:11 explains that ignorance can have a damaging impact on you, which can consequently affect those connected to you. The word "ignorant in 2 Corinthians 2:11 is the Greek word 'agnoeo,' that refers to one's ignorance or lack of certain facts. However, it also includes making mistakes or errors due to lack of understanding. It is the picture of an uneducated person who due to a lack of knowledge, is prone to arriving at mistaken conclusion or destination. The word 'agnoeo' depicts someone who is in the dark or without a clue. Because this

person lacks understanding, his conclusion and destination are faulty, erroneous, and misguided. This is where we get the word agnostic; the official name used to describe individuals who claim they don't know what they believe. So, when someone claims to be agnostic, he is claiming to be ignorant.

An example of this kind of ignorance is often seen when a person is diagnosed with terminal disease sent from the devil, yet he believes that his sickness came from God, possibly as a retribution or a divine lesson of life. Because the sick person is ignorant of the fact that God is not the author of sickness and disease but Satan, he mistakenly concludes that his sickness must be God's will for his life. This ignorance is so devastating that it could lead to that individual's premature death. Do you see how dangerous it is to remain ignorant of how the devil operates? He viciously came to kill, to steal and ultimately to destroy. We must confront and subdue him with the truth.

"Then you will know the truth, and the truth will set you free"(John 8:32 NIV).

> *"The thief's purpose is to steal and kill and destroy. My purpose is to give them a rich and satisfying life" (John 10:10).*

I have seen servants upon horses, and princes walking as servants upon the earth. We are a chosen generation called forth to show His excellence according to Scriptures.

> *"But you are a chosen people, a royal priesthood, a holy nation, a people belonging to God, that you may declare the praises of him who called you out of darkness into his wonderful light" (1 Peter 2:9 NIV).*

> *"Everything that goes into a life of pleasing God has been miraculously given to us by getting to know, personally and intimately, the One who invited us to God. The best invitation we ever received! We were also given absolutely terrific promises to pass on to you -your tickets to participation in the life of God after you turned your back on the world corrupted by lust"*
> *(2 Peter 1:3-4 TMB).*

Destiny

Your destiny is where you are heading to, or where you ought to be or arrived at in this life. Often, people interchange purpose with destiny. Your purpose is decided and designed by God, but your destiny is determined by yourself alone through the choices you make now. It depends on the choices and decisions you make in life. However, your divine destiny is the appointed place that God has designed for you to fulfill all your divine assignments, (purpose or call) in life, without struggling.

In the book of 2 Samuel 7:10, God promised the Children of Israel an appointed place, permanently for them. This is the place of permanent ownership, divinely secured and stabilized, a place they will experience divine immunity and flourish supernaturally in all endeavors of life. It is a place of divine establishment for His people.

"Moreover I will appoint a place for My people Israel, and will plant them, that they

may dwell in a place of their own and move no more; nor shall the sons of wickedness oppress them anymore, as previously" (2 Samuel 7:10).

You must understand that your God-given vision requires a functional presence of God in your life, and God's guidance in whatever you do in the process. Furthermore, you have to consciously let go of your past negative life experiences, and release your untapped potentials for the assignment ahead. These are crucial and relevant to fulfilling your divine destiny.

> *"Do not remember the former things,*
> *Nor consider the things of old"*
> *(Isa 43:18, NKJV).*

Understanding Your Divine Calling And Purpose

Chapter 3

Defining The Call

The Call is God's sovereign selection of individuals of any race, status or gender (male/female), to participate in His universal program for humanity. The Call is the reason why the person who is called is created for and exists. The Call is a strong and an unwavering desire to be committed to a specific work or task such as a kingdom assignment. Interestingly, in every generation God will always at His discretion, call certain people for specific tasks.

Who Is Called?

Typically, God is not looking for aristocrats, those of high social status, the ruling class, the nobility, those with influence and money, the highly educated and in some cases politically influential. Though, He can use them if He decides to do so, as I have indicated earlier, but He rarely does.

> *"For ye see your calling brethren, how that not many wise men after the flesh, not many mighty, not many noble, are called."* *(1 Corinthians 1:26).*

God Is Looking For The Foolish Things Of The World

God has consistently chosen people that the world does not reckon with but regarded as nonentities to accomplish great things on earth. Like I have stated earlier, looking at world history and the consistency of the Scriptures, you will realize that God does not consider the social status of individuals as a precondition for calling them into the ministry. The aforementioned explains why He rarely uses the cream and upper class of the society to advance His Kingdom purpose on earth, even though He can if He decides to. God had indeed used some in that class, no doubt.

> *"But God has chosen the foolish things of the world to put to shame the wise, and God has chosen the weak things of the world to put to shame the things which are mighty; and the base things of the world and the things which are despised God has chosen, and the things which are not, to bring to nothing the things that are, that no flesh should glory in His presence" (1 Corinthians 1:27-29).*

From the onset of time as it were, God has always reached into the hearts of ordinary men and women to accomplish great feats by His grace and power working through them to establish His plans on earth.

> *"Behold, I am the Lord, the God of all flesh. Is there anything too hard for Me?" (Jeremiah 32:27).*

What Is The Qualification To Be Called?

God looks at deep within our hearts, not our accomplishments.

> *"For the eyes of the Lord run to and fro throughout the whole earth, to show Himself strong on behalf of those whose heart is loyal to Him. In this you have done foolishly; therefore, from now on you shall have wars"* (2 Chronicles 16 :9 NKJV).

It would be foolish to overlook the fact that many intelligent men and women who loved God have also made great impacts in the world, over the years. Apostle Paul was part of this elite group before he came to know Christ. Apollos, Paul's friend who pastored the church at Corinth also came from this elite class of his days. But Paul and Apollos were not typical of the first-century ministers of the Gospel.

By no means am I demeaning education. I encourage people to get as much education as possible, but school issued pieces of paper in the name of certificates or diploma as some may call it, are not the criteria that impress God and gets His attention. There have been many educated people who God could not use for His divine purpose. Even though they were brilliant according to the flesh, they were not worthy of being chosen because their hearts were not right before God.

> *"But the Lord said to Samuel, "Do not look at his appearance or at his physical stature, because I have refused him. For the Lord does not see as man sees; for man looks at the outward appearance, but the Lord looks at the heart" (1 Sam 16:7 NKJV).*

Education may help you to get a good job and positively sway the opinion of men in your favor, but Paul makes it clear that God is not bent on using "brilliance" according to the standard of this world.

According to worldly standards, it would have been better for Jesus the Son of God to have been born in a palace, with a gold-gilded wall and floor, with trumpets and cymbals blasting to announce His birth.

Therefore, if you have ever thought you were not good enough for God to use, it's time for you to renew your thinking (mind). God is looking for people no one else wants or deems worthy to be used.

Whenever an ordinary person accomplishes notable achievements, there is no question as to who should receive the glory. Conversely, the upper-class individuals tend to arrogate the glory to themselves when they accomplish great successes. It becomes questionable as to who gets the glory.

1 Corinthians 1:29 says,
"That no flesh should glory in His presence."

The Old and New Testaments are filled with illustrations of people whom God wanted, but the world rejected. God's choice is not based on beauty or ugliness, talent or lack of talent, education or lack of education, a diploma or lack of diploma, degrees or lack of degrees. None of these can move God.

If a person has a right heart toward God, he is a qualified candidate to be used by Him at any time to do great exploits for Him.

> *"For the eyes of the Lord run to and fro throughout the whole earth, to show Himself strong on behalf of those whose heart is loyal to Him. In this you have done foolishly; therefore, from now on you shall have wars" (2 Chronicles 16:9 NKJV).*

Where Are You Called To?

Every call or ministry has a geographical location. We read in Acts 1:8 that the Disciples knew their calling was to witness for Christ in Jerusalem, Judea, Samaria, and unto the uttermost part of the earth, Similarly. In the book of Galatians1:21-22, we saw that Paul knew where to do ministry in the regions of Syria and Cilicia. As he responded accordingly, he was effective and made a distinguished impact.

God has always shown up in places where He wasn't expected. Consider the location where Jesus was born, in a lowly shepherd's stall. This certainly was not the place anyone would have expected the King of kings to be born, but God chose the foolish things to confound the wise.

> *"Afterward I went into the regions of Syria and Cilicia. And I was unknown by face to the churches of Judea which were in Christ" (Galatians 1:21-22 NKJV).*

Who Are You Called To?

Paul was specifically sent to the Gentiles as we read in Acts 26:17, 2 Corinthians 10:13-16. When Jesus sent the seventy disciples, He described to them who to go to and who not to go to. I pray that you discover who you are sent to in Jesus' name.

> *"After these things the Lord appointed seventy others also, and sent them two by two before His face into every city and place where He Himself was about to go" (Luke 10:1-2 NKJV).*

How Do You Respond To The Call?

We must find out from Him who called us to show us the way. Jesus showed the disciples how they should do ministry.

> *"On one occasion, while he was eating with them, he gave them this command: "Do not leave Jerusalem, but wait for the gift my Father promised, which you have heard me speak about. ... But you will receive power when the Holy Spirit comes on you; and you will be my witnesses in Jerusalem, and in all Judea and Samaria, and to the ends of the earth" (Acts 1:4-8 NIV).*

How to Fulfill Your God Given Purpose

> *"For we are God's handiwork, created in Christ Jesus to do good works, which God prepared in advance for us to do"*
> *(Ephesians 2:10 NIV).*

It's easy to get caught up in the greatness of everyone else's lives. Obviously, we see all of the lovely moments our acquaintances share on social media. We surely rejoice with our closest friends when a baby is born, or when that long-awaited promotion comes through. If you're wondering when your special moments will take place, you're probably too immersed in the lives around you to realize the beauty that is already upon your life.

In Ephesians 2, we see that God has prepared in advance good works for us to accomplish. God uniquely crafted you for a purpose! He isn't just passing to you the leftover blessings that someone else rejected or even abandoned. He has marvelous plans specially set aside for you before you were born. You have a unique calling on your life, which means your glorious moments may not look exactly like those around you.

You may have an amazing ability to create things – whether it's art, music, movies, or stories. Still, you're wondering why you're not a wife or a husband like your best friend or why you didn't go to school to become a doctor like the person you are admiring.

While you're busy portraying yourself into someone else's story, you're failing to see your unique purpose by disregarding what you were delicately fashioned to do by God.

No one enjoys putting pieces of puzzle together only to discover at the end that one piece is missing. You are an imperative and priceless piece of God's puzzle. Let's hone in on what we were created to conquer so that we can complete the beautiful picture He had laid out for us, even before we were born.

I encourage you to meditate on the things that give your heart unspeakable joy. Ask God how to use those passions to serve others and to perform the divine assignment set aside that only you can complete.

How to Fulfill Your God Given Purpose Through Preparation

Apart from divine direction, we must be a people of preparation. Preparation is an action or process of making something ready for use or service. It is getting ready for some random test or duty. The preparation process is essential for securing promotion in our lives and entering into our destiny. Times invested in preparation is never a wasted time. The preparatory seasons in your life are not delays to your future success. Each chapter and season of your life have a duty to accomplish and dividend to reap from if you will look for them.

(Mike Murdock: The Leadership Secrets of Jesus 61)

Don't Assume or Speculate

In ministry, you don't go to war with another man's armor, like Saul tempted David to do. The reason being that the armor was not designed to fit David. In fact, it's a misfit for the young David. Therefore, he refused to put on King Saul's armor for the battle. He wanted to go at his own pace and remain on own his side of the battlefield. Be yourself, the original you. Don't ever attempt to be a duplicate of others. Your calling and purpose is unique.

"And Saul armed David with his armour, and he put an helmet of brass upon his head; also he armed him with a coat of mail. And David girded his sword upon his armour, and he assayed to go; for he had not proved it. And David said unto Saul, I cannot go with these; for I have not proved them. And David put them off him" (1 Sam. 17:38-39).

Preparation is an "action or the process of making something ready for use or service. It's getting ready for occasion, examinations, test or duty" according to the definition of *(Merriam-Webster, Online Dictionary).*

It is unwise and a delusion to think that we will experience success without deliberately investing the time of preparation. It has been said that success occurs when opportunity meets with preparation.

Abraham Lincoln made this statement about his philosophy of life: *"I will get ready and then perhaps my chance will come" (Moncur).* Great time of preparation results in great opportunities.

John Maxwell made an interesting statement regarding the process of preparation.

"God prepares leaders in a crock-pot, not in a microwave oven. More important than the awaited goal is the work God does in us whiles we wait. Waiting deepens and matures us, levels our perspectives, and broadens our understanding. Tests of time determine whether we can endure seasons of seemingly unfruitful preparation, and indicate whether we can recognize and seize the opportunities that come our way." **(The Maxwell Leadership Bible 66).**

Chapter 4

What Comes With The Calling?

There are levels of suffering, sacrifice, lose and death that come with the purpose or call of God in our lives. The calling of God upon the Apostles' lives resulted in some levels of sufferings, even unto death. Ultimately, they all suffered a shameful and disgraceful death.

Perhaps this is a reminder to us that our sufferings here are indeed minor compared to the intense persecution and cold cruelty faced by the early Apostles and Disciples during their times for the sake of their faith in Jesus Christ.

> *"And ye shall be hated of all men for my name's sake: But he that endureth to the end shall be saved" (Matthew 10:22).*

Please let's be encouraged that Christianity is not for the timid but the bold and audacious. In other words, Christianity can transform the fearful to the daring.

Examples of Daring Christians Offered as Sacrifices for the Kingdom

Matthew suffered martyrdom in Ethiopia, killed by a sword.

Mark died in Alexandria, Egypt, after being dragged by horses through the streets until he was dead.

Luke died by hanging in Greece because of his fiery preaching of the Gospel of Jesus Christ to the lost.

John faced martyrdom like the other Apostles and was thrown in a huge basin of boiling oil during a wave of persecution in Rome. However, he was miraculously delivered from death and finally received the greatest revelation ever in the history of humanity.

Afterward, the Roman Empire confined him to the mines on the prison Island of Patmos, where he received the revelation of Jesus Christ through an angel sent by God.

He wrote the prophetic Book of Revelation on the Island of Patmos. Apostle John was later freed and returned to serve as Bishop of Edessa in modern Turkey. He died as an old man full of age. He was the only Apostle to die a natural and peaceful death.

Peter was crucified on an x-shaped cross upside down. According to church tradition, it was because he told his tormentors that he felt unworthy to die in the same way that Jesus Christ died.

James, the leader of the Church in Jerusalem, was thrown over a hundred feet down from the southeast pinnacle of the Temple when he refused to deny his faith in Christ. When they discovered that he survived the fall, his enemies beat him to death with a fuller's club. (This was the same pinnacle where Satan had taken Jesus during the Temptation at the wilderness).

James, the Son of Zebedee, was a fisherman by trade when Jesus called him to a lifetime of ministry. As a strong leader of the church, James was ultimately beheaded at Jerusalem. The Roman officer who guarded James watched in amazement as James defended his faith at his trial. Later, the officer walked beside James to the place of execution. Overcome by conviction, he declared his new faith in Jesus Christ to the judge and knelt beside James to accept being beheading as a Christian.

Bartholomew also known as Nathaniel was a missionary to Asia. He witnessed for our

Lord in present day Turkey. Bartholomew was martyred for his preaching in Armenia where he was flayed to death by a whip.

Andrew was crucified on an x-shaped cross in Patras, Greece. After being whipped severely by seven soldiers, they tied his body to the cross with cords to prolong his agony. His followers reported that when he was led toward the cross, Andrew saluted it in these words: 'I have long desired and expected this happy hour. The cross has been consecrated by the body of Christ hanging on it.' He continued to preach to his tormentors for two days until he finally died.

Thomas was stabbed with a spear in India during one of his missionary trips to establish the church in the Sub-Continent.

Jude was killed with arrows when he refused to deny his faith in Christ.

Matthias, chosen to replace the traitor Judas Iscariot, was stoned and then beheaded.

Paul was tortured and then beheaded by the evil Emperor Nero at Rome in A.D. 67. Paul endured a lengthy imprisonment in Rome, which allowed him to write his many Epistles to the churches he planted throughout the Roman Empire. These letters, which taught the believers then many of the foundational Doctrines of Christianity, form a large portion of the New Testament Scriptures.

Matthew 10: 22 tells us,
> *"And ye shall be hated of all men for my name's sake: but he that endureth to the end shall be saved."*

They are levels of suffering that every follower of Jesus must endure.

> *"If anyone comes to me and does not hate father and mother, wife and children, brothers and sisters—yes, even their own life—such a person cannot be my disciple" (Luke 14:26 NIV).*

They are three levels of sufferings God allows Christian leaders to endure for the sake of the Kingdom of God.

1. **They Bleed**
2. **They Sweat as Blood**
3. **They Shed Tears That No One Sees**

Obviously, God allows and enables them to pass through these painful experiences for the sake of the Kingdom. Their understanding of the truth that God will not allow what they can't bear come their way, can be comforting in such moments of trials in their lives.

> *"No temptation has overtaken you except such as is common to man; but God is faithful, who will not allow you to be tempted beyond what you are able, but with the temptation will also make the way of escape, that you may be able to bear it" (1Corinthians 10:13NKJV).*

The people God allows to see their experiences of suffering are members of their families:

God Himself: He sees them in their most secret places of pains, agony, and isolation, and supernaturally comforts them. This spiritual comfort enables them to carry on till the end.

Their Spouses: They see them but does not complain. They rather encourage them to press on and emotionally bear the burden with them.

Their Children: They bear it with honor, dignity, and glory, even when it is hurting.

It takes apostolic mantle to say these things and the Issachar anointing to discern them.

No Comparison Just Be The Original You

> *"For you see your calling, brethren, that not many wise according to the flesh, not many mighty, not many noble, are called. But God has chosen the foolish things of the*

world to put to shame the wise, and God has chosen the weak things of the world to put to shame the things which are mighty; and the base things of the world and the things which are despised God has chosen, and the things which are not, to bring to nothing the things that are, that no flesh should glory in His presence. But of Him you are in Christ Jesus, who became for us wisdom from God and righteousness and sanctification and redemption that, as it is written, "He who glories, let him glory in the Lord" (1Corinthians 26-31).

God in His infinite wisdom, selected people who are nonentities in the world's view, not from high ranking families or the upper echelon of society.

In fact, the world sees them as imbeciles, jerks, real twerps yet God is using them to utterly confound those who seem smart in the eyes of the world.

So, if God is not looking for the upper class of the society, He must be looking to the lowly class as stratified by human standards. He has been using the ordinary, usual, regular, routine, run-of-the-mill, standard, typical kind of people. This means that if you come from a lowly or average background, you are possibly the very candidate God wants to use. Don't count yourself out, if God has not.

Obviously, God has called the rich and famous as well, but it is the regular folks who most often find themselves chosen by God to carry out His purpose on earth. He specializes in using ordinary people like you and me. That is what Paul goes on to say in 1 Corinthians 1:2.

> *"But God hath chosen the foolish things of the world to confound the wise..." The truth is that no one is an idiot in God's view, but the world often views people whom God chooses as being nitwits, lamebrains, and idiots."*

What has God decreed about your life?

- You are not disadvantaged, regardless of where you came from

- Purpose is discovered and fulfilled by decrees and not by degrees

"Before I formed thee in the belly I knew thee; and before thou camest forth out of the womb I sanctified thee, and I ordained thee a prophet unto the nations. Then said I, Ah, Lord GOD! behold, I cannot speak: for I am a child. But the LORD said unto me, say not, I am a child: for thou shalt go to all that I shall send thee, and whatsoever I command thee thou shalt speak. Be not afraid of their faces: for I am with thee to deliver thee, saith the LORD" (Jeremiah 1:5-8).

If you consider yourself as weak, feeble or unskilled, don't let that bother you at all. God has been calling feeble and unskilled people from the beginning of time. Few of those whom God has called have been "the nobility" according to the flesh. Repeatedly, God has chosen people who were lightly esteemed by the standards of the world for a divine assignment here on earth.

"For my thoughts are not your thoughts, neither are your ways my ways, saith the LORD"(Isaiah 55:8).

God Doesn't Call The Wise

The call of God is a special invitation to a person to do some particular work designed to extend the Kingdom of God and bless humanity. Therefore, the call of God is what He has destined one to be and do in His Kingdom. In other words, it is God who has placed a call on your life. If at any time, you get confused and perplexed about the call, don't hesitate to go back to Him for explanation and revelation of what to do at such confusing moments in your life.

Repeatedly I have said that God doesn't call many who are considered 'wise' by the world. The word 'wise' is from the Greek word 'Sophos, which refers to a person who possesses a special enlightenment or insight. It portrays a clever, smart, astute, intellectually brilliant and super impressive above the rest of society. It depicts people who are highly educated, like scientists, philosophers, doctors, teachers and many others who are considered super-intelligent human beings.

Questions

Can you recall some examples of people in the Bible whom the world thought to worth nothing, yet God called them, changed them and used them to change world history?

Try to name five people who fit into this category. Can you think of particular people besides those in the Bible whom the world thought worth next to nothing, yet God used them to change society? Try to name five people who fit this category as well.

If God specializes in calling people who come from common backgrounds, what does this mean for you? This was explained by God to these men in the next page.

Read and Study These Bible References

1. Noah in-Genesis 6:13-14, 22

2. Abram in Genesis 12:1-3

3. Moses in Exodus 3:1-2, 7, 10

5. Gideon in Judges 6:12-14

6. Samuel in1 Samuel 3:6-8

7. David in 1 Samuel 13:1, 12-13

8. Jeremiah in Jeremiah 1:4-5

9. Joseph was called through dreams to be the preserver and savior of God's people in Egypt, during a global famine (Gen. 45:5-8)

10. Samson and John the Baptist were called from the womb to be God's servants. Their parents received the call by Angelic visitation (Judges 13 and Luke 1 respectively).

11. Jesus called two brothers - James and John, sons of Zebedee (Matt. 4:18) and a tax collector - Matthew or Levi (Matt. 9:9).

12. Another person with a peculiar calling was Saul, who later became known as Paul, who recounted his testimony in Acts 26:13-16.

The purpose of the five-fold ministry gifts is to build and mature the Body of Christ into the full stature and image of Christ to do ministry in everyday life outside of the four walls of the church. Every believer in Christ is a potential minister of the Gospel and an ambassador of Christ.

> *"And He Himself gave some to be apostles, some prophets, some evangelists, and some pastors and teachers, for the equipping of the saints for the work of ministry, for the edifying of the body of Christ, till we all come to the unity of the faith and of the knowledge of the Son of God, to a perfect man, to the measure of the stature of the fullness of Christ" (Ephesians 4:11-13 NKJV).*

Understanding Your Divine Calling And Purpose

Chapter 5

You Are Not An Accident

> *"Just as He chose us in Him before the foundation of the world, that we would be holy and blameless before Him. In love" (Ephesians 1:4).*

It is interesting to know that God chose us even before we were born. Often you hear people say "my parents did not plan to have me. I was accidentally born and no one expected me" This group of individuals use the circumstances surrounding their birth as an excuse for not accepting their responsibilities in life. They regard and label themselves as products of parental mistakes. Unfortunately, this predisposition puts them in a severely disadvantaged position in life. It consequently robs them of the aspirations to thrive and succeed in life. Sadly, most of them end up not living a meaningful and significant life.

Friend, listen to me, I want you to know that even though you may have been a surprise to your parents, you were never a surprise to God. The Bible makes it expressly clear that long before we were ever conceived in our mothers' wombs, God already knew us and earmarked a unique purpose for each of us to accomplish during our lifetime on earth. According to Jeremiah 1:5, God called us to be His Children with a special purpose to accomplish in this world. Jeremiah was called as a prophet to the nations at his time.

> *"Before I formed you in the womb I knew you, and before you were born I consecrated you; I have appointed you a prophet to the nations" (Jeremiah 1:5).*

In Psalm 139:15-16, David declares that God's eyes were fixed on us not only when we were in the earliest stages of being formed in our mother's womb, but even before we were conceived. David said this concerning himself and us today.

> *"My substance was not hid from thee, when I was made in secret, and curiously wrought in the lowest parts of the earth. Thine eyes did see my substance, yet being unperfect; and in thy book all my members were written, which in continuance were fashioned, when as yet there was none of them."*

According to David, God knew us when we were nothing more than mere "substance" in the earliest stages of being formed in our mothers' wombs. He was so intricately aware of us that He looked, as our arms, hands, fingers, legs, feet, and toes were being formed. In fact, this verse says He even knew us, and by faith, He could see us being conceived, formed, and born into this world. This means there isn't a single human being on the earth who is a surprise to God, and that includes you. To further expatiate on what David was saying, I have added three more translations of the Bible verses for deeper understanding.

> *"You know me inside and out, you know every bone in my body; You know exactly how I was made, bit by bit, how I was sculpted from nothing into something. Like an open book, you watched me grow from concep-tion to birth; all the stages of my life were spread out before you, the days of my life all prepared before I'd even lived one day" (Psalms 139:15-16TMB).*

> *"My bones were not hidden from you when I was being made in secret, intricately woven in the depths of the earth. Your eyes could see me as an embryo, but in your book, all my days were already written; my days had been shaped before any of them existed" (Psalms 139:15-16 CJB).*

> *"You saw my bones being formed as I took shape in my mother's body. When I was put*

together there, you saw my body as it was formed. All the days planned for me were written in your book before I was one day old" (Psalms 139:15-16 NCV).

Even as believers we were saved by design, not by accident. Paul writes, *"According as he hath chosen us in him before the foundation of the world..."* The word "chosen" in Greek is 'eklego' a compound of the words 'ek' and 'lego.' The word 'ek' means 'out,' and the word 'lego' means 'I say.' Together these words mean 'Out, I say'! It can also mean to call out, to select, to elect, or to personally choose. God intentionally begot us into His eternal and heavenly family.

In classical Greek writings, this word 'eklego' refers to a person or group of people who were selected for a particular purpose. For example, the word 'eklego' was used for the selection of men for military service. It was also used to distinguish selected soldiers who were chosen out of the entire military to go on a special mission or to do a special task. Finally, it was used to describe politicians who were elected by the general consensus to hold a public office or to execute a special assignment on behalf of the community.

In every case where the word 'eklego' is used to portray the election or selection of individuals, it conveys the idea of the great privilege and honor of being chosen. It also strongly speaks of the responsibility placed on those who are chosen to walk, act, and live in a manner that is honorable to their calling. Because of the great privilege of being elected to a higher position or selected to perform a special task, those who are "chosen" bear the responsibility to walk and act in accordance with the calling that has been extended to them. They should look upon themselves as chosen, honored, esteemed, and respected as special representatives of the one who elected them. What a privilege.

So, when Paul says in Ephesians chapter 1 that God hath chosen us in Him before the foundation of the world..., he's saying that God looked out to the horizon of human history and saw us. His voice echoed from heaven: "Out, I say!" In that flesh (our lives), destinies were divinely sealed. We were separated by God from a lost and dying world, and called us as co-laborers in the Kingdom to be His own special people.

> *"But you are a chosen race, a priesthood of kingly lineage, a holy nation, a people belonging specially to God, that you may make known the perfections of Him who called you out of darkness into His marvelous light" (1 Peter 2:9 Weymouth).*

Just as the word 'eklego' in classical Greek depicted the military selection of young men to leave their homes and serve in the military, God looked out at the entire human race and personally selected, elected, and especially chose us to come away from the world and be permanently enlisted as His sons and daughters. Now as children of the

King, we bear the awesome responsibility of walking worthily of the high calling we have received and demonstrate it to the world.

"That you may walk worthy of the Lord, fully pleasing Him, being fruitful in every good work and increasing in the knowledge of God" (Colossians 1:10-11 NKJV).

Look at when this selection took place. Paul says it occurred "... before the foundation of the world...." The word "foundation" is the Greek word 'katabole,' a compound of the words 'kata' and 'bole.' The word 'kata' means down, and the word 'bole' means to hurl or to throw. These two words together mean to forcibly hurl something down, and it refers to the act of creation. Thus, before God ever spoke the earth into existence, before His booming voice ever called out the first layers of the earth's crust to be put into place, He had already spoken our names. He selected and elected us before the very first layers of the earth were created.

Considering the Greek meaning of 'katabole', Ephesians 1:4 could be phrased to read as:

> *"When God saw us, He said, 'Out, I say!' In that moment, He separated us from the rest of the world and enlisted us in His service. And think of it! He did all of this before He ever hurled the first layers of the earth's crust into existence…."*

Therefore, if your flesh ever tries to rant and rave that you're not worthy enough to be used of God or that you're an accident, you need to take authority over your flesh and shut its mouth. Then declare to your flesh that "God chose me and planned a great future for me. He wants to use me." I'm not going to listen anymore to those negative words from my lying flesh and unrenewed mind and emotions. I have an awesome destiny. In fact, I'm a significant part of God's grand plan."

Stop listening to your filthy, stinking, lying, fibbing flesh. God has been waiting for your arrival for a very long time! It's time for you to accept His assignment and make the necessary changes to flow with His purpose for your life. He has been calling out to you all the time, saying, "my beloved, get up and jump in the race. I want you. I'm calling you to be part of my winning team."

There is too much at stake for you to make the mistake of sitting around feeling sorry for yourself. You can only begin to experience true significance when you accept the fact that God has chosen you. Then you can begin to live up to the glorious calling He has placed on your life. Regardless of how big or small the assignment, joy and satisfaction will be yours when you start accomplishing what God brought you into this world to do for His glory, and for the benefit of others. This is what imparts true significance to any person's life. No satisfaction compares with this kind of satisfaction.

Those who contribute nothing meaningful to life are usually the ones who consistently struggle with the sense of purposelessness. Conversely, intentional living will help you to overcome the trap and deceit of living a life of without purpose.

Even if you think your gifts are insignificant in comparison to others, you can still use them to make a difference in life. If you use the gifts God gave you, they will develop further. The more proficient you become at using those gifts, the more valuable you will become to the larger society. On the other hand, you will inadvertently cause your life to be inconsequential if you ignore them. God gave them to you to make the most of the life assignment He has entrusted to you.

If you contribute nothing positive to this world, your entire life becomes pointless and insignificant. Don't let that describe your life. God didn't bring you into the world so you would live a pointless and inconsequential life. He has a purpose for your life. He wants to use you. He wants you to be a significant part of His grandeurs plan. It is up to you to either respond or remain where you are and complain all through life.

> *"If you'll willingly obey, you'll feast like kings. But if you're willful and stubborn, you'll die like dogs. "That's right. God says so" (Isa 1:19-20 TMB).*

CONCLUSION

Change The Channel

A life that is governed by purpose is a life of significance. Conversely, a purposeless life is an insignificant life. "The greatest tragedy in life is not death, but a life without a purpose." - **Dr. Myles Munroe.**

Life is like a television with a remote control. If you don't like the channel, change it. If you don't like the way life is treating you, change the way you treat life. If you do not like the way people have been treating you, change the way you act and treat others. I learned a long time ago that I can change myself faster than I can ever change anyone else.

I cannot remain depressed when I think about the glory of accomplishing God's purpose for my life, and His goodness that I have experienced in the process, so far. The greatest discovery you can make in life is the discovery of your God-given purpose. "If purpose is not known, abuse is inevitable" - **Dr. Myles Munroe.**

Unfortunately, there are lots of people today whose lives are subject to all forms of abuse because of lack of understanding of God's purpose for their lives. If you belong to this category, I have written this book to end that misery in your life and in the life of someone reading this book today.

The devil hates a smile on your face. He will lure you to frown at life if you allow him. He wants to cast a cloud of doom over every thought, relationship, and situations in your life if you do not resist him. Therefore, change the channel of your life today, and resist the devil in everything you say and do. *"Submit yourselves therefore to God, resist the devil, and He will flee from you." James 4:7*. You have to understand the wiles of the enemy and rebuke his temptations at every point in your day-to-day life.

"Solid character will reflect itself in consistent behavior, while poor character will seek to hide behind deceptive words and actions." - **Dr. Myles Munroe.**

"You must decide if you are going to rob the world or bless it with the rich, valuable, potent, and untapped resources locked away within you." - **Dr. Myles Munroe**, *Understanding Your Potential.*

Finally, I want to thank and acknowledge our brothers Dr. Myles Munroe of blessed memory for his deep revelation on the subject of purpose, as I referenced him in this book, and also Rick Renner for his depth of knowledge of the Greek language. Most of the Greek references and translations used in this book are quoted from his book *"Sparkling Gems From The Greek."* Beside the Greek references, some of his online teachings is part of the resources I used as well. I also referenced some other sources; *rickrenner.org, powwrofthecross.net, biblegateway.com goodreads.com, crosswork.com,* to substantiate and bring a balance to the subject matter of the book.

www.ingramcontent.com/pod-product-compliance
Lightning Source LLC
Chambersburg PA
CBHW050612100526
44584CB00038B/3057